Mama's Rules for Livin'

by
Mamie McCullough

HONOR
BOOKS

Tulsa, Oklahoma

Unless otherwise indicated, all Scripture quotations are taken from the *Holy Bible: New International Version®*. NIV®. Copyright © 1973, 1978, 1984 by International Bible Society. Used by permission of Zondervan Publishing House. All rights reserved.

5th Printing

Mama's Rules for Livin'
ISBN 1-56292-085-5
Copyright © 1995 by Mamie McCullough
305 Spring Creek Village, Box 372
Dallas, Texas 75248

Published by Honor Books, Inc.
P.O. Box 55388
Tulsa, Oklahoma 74155

Printed in the United States of America. All rights reserved under International Copyright Law. Contents and/or cover may not be reproduced in whole or in part in any form without the express written consent of the Publisher.

Presented to

_____

Presented by

_____

Date

_____

Introduction

We all need rules and regulations in order to grow into healthy individuals. As children, these are handed down to us by our parents or significant others. I was fortunate to have had a wonderful mother who was not formally educated, but who had much wisdom. Mother raised me, my five sisters, and my three brothers on four basic rules:

- **Go to Church**
- **Love Others**
- **Stay Clean**
- **Work Hard**

As I have raised my three children, these have been the "unwritten" rules for my home as well.

If you are a person who has not had a good and caring parent, it does not mean *you* cannot be a good parent. Decide what values and ideals you want to instill in your children, then live them.

I believe most parenting problems stem from not making the decision on **how** to live.

The ideas in this book have worked for me, and I believe because they are "basic child raising" they will work for you too.

Mamie McCullough

*D*on't just go through life

grow through life.

····*Mama's Rules for Livin'*····

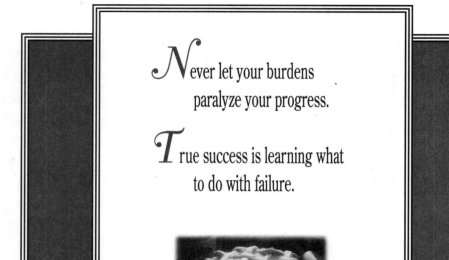

*N*ever let your burdens
paralyze your progress.

*T*rue success is learning what
to do with failure.

····*Mama's Rules for Livin'*····

*N*o matter what you've

done...I believe in you!

We make our habits, then
in turn our habits make us.

Little things make a big
difference.

····*Mama's Rules for Livin'*····

$\mathcal{Y}$ou were created with the

seeds of greatness —

be all you can be.

*W*inners develop the habit of

doing those things that

losers refuse to do.

*R*emember, work is not

a punishment but an

antidote...never quit!

G et rid of the "Yeah, buts."

I f you don't know how
to do something — START.

*T*he man who moves

mountains begins by

carrying away small

stones.

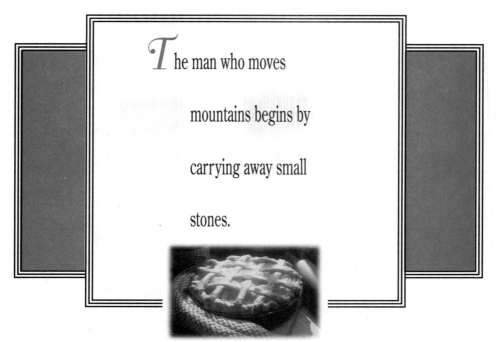

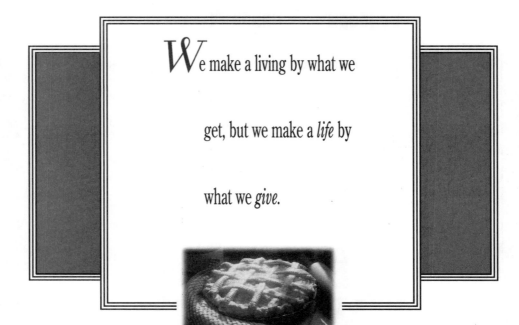

We make a living by what we

get, but we make a *life* by

what we *give*.

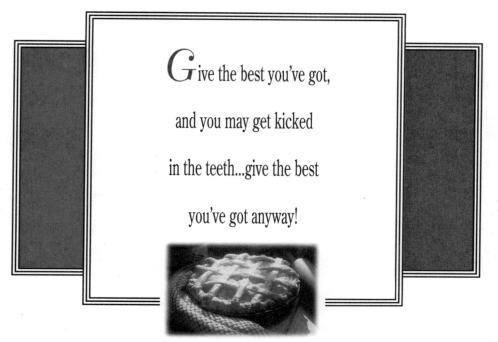

Give the best you've got,

and you may get kicked

in the teeth...give the best

you've got anyway!

*P*eople don't plan to fail —
they fail to plan.

*G*oals are dreams with
deadlines.

·····*Mama's Rules for Livin'*·····

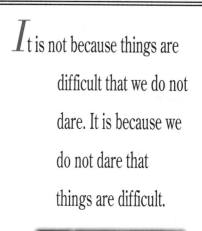

*I*t is not because things are
difficult that we do not
dare. It is because we
do not dare that
things are difficult.

*I*t isn't the load that weights

you down — it's the way

you carry it.

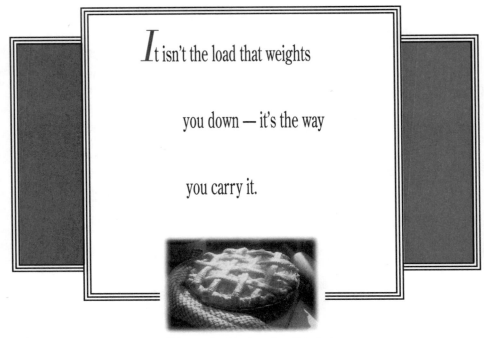

····*Mama's Rules for Livin'*····

I can do everything through

him who gives me strength.

Philippians 4:13

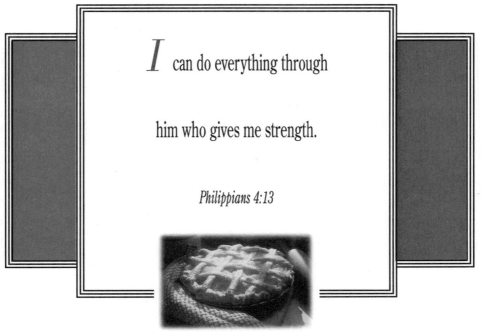

*I*t is never right to do wrong.

*I*t is never wrong to do right.

·····*Mama's Rules for Livin'*·····

*C*haracter is doing what is

right — on purpose!

A person wrapped up

in himself makes a

very small package.

·····*Mama's Rules for Livin'*·····

When you become a parent

remember: Children are sent

through us — not to us.

*Y*ou do not have to like
everything a person does
in order to love him.

*R*espect the rights, customs,
and differences of others.

····*Mama's Rules for Livin'*····

$\mathcal{B}$e a goodfinder — look for

the good in others.

*T*alking is sharing.

*L*istening is caring.

·····*Mama's Rules for Livin'*·····

$\mathcal{Y}$ou can give without loving,

but you cannot love

without giving.

*I*f you want to be an original,

be yourself.

·····*Mama's Rules for Livin'*·····

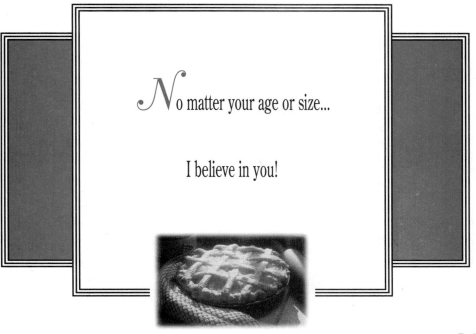

$\mathcal{N}$o matter your age or size...

I believe in you!

God does not promise to leave
us comfortable, but He will
never leave us comfortless.

Faith is seeing a rainbow
in each tear.

·····*Mama's Rules for Livin'*·····

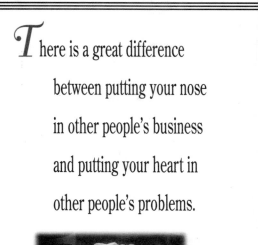

*T*here is a great difference
between putting your nose
in other people's business
and putting your heart in
other people's problems.

Winners are not

"why-ners."

·····*Mama's Rules for Livin'*·····

$\mathcal{E}$ven when the odds seem

against you...never quit!

*A*s we see people, so we tend
to treat them.

*A*s we treat people,
often they become.

*D*iscipline others in private

and praise them in public.

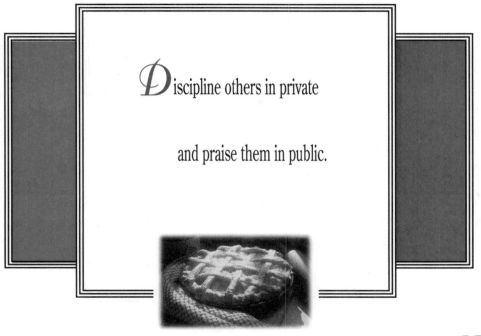

*S*uccess is measured by how many people you have helped.

····*Mama's Rules for Livin'*····

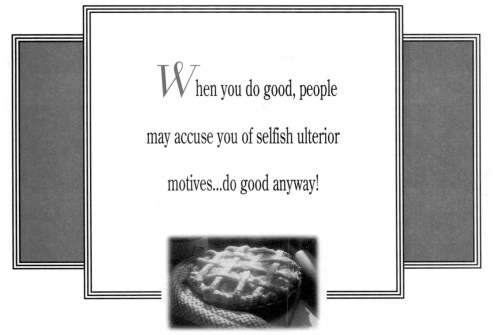

When you do good, people

may accuse you of selfish ulterior

motives...do good anyway!

When you sling mud,
you're just losing ground.

Simplify your life — shake
off the hurt, bitterness,
and bad feelings.

····*Mama's Rules for Livin'*····

*T*he only people to get

even with are those who

have helped you.

When your heart is right,

God will make your

head right.

·····*Mama's Rules for Livin'*·····

*I*n all your ways acknowledge

him, and he will make

your paths straight.

Proverbs 3:6

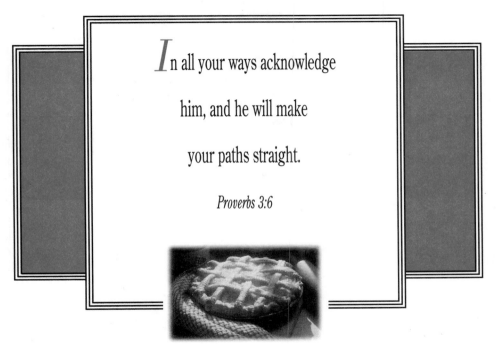

····*Mama's Rules for Livin'*····

*D*o not complain about
what you permit.

*T*ake steps to overcome
your failures.

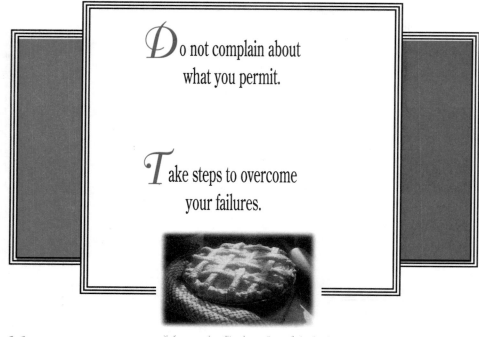

····*Mama's Rules for Livin'*····

*I*n the presence of trouble,

be a person who grows

wings, not a person who

buys crutches.

*S*tay alert for opportunity.

····*Mama's Rules for Livin'*····

When you become a parent
remember: To be in your children's
memories tomorrow, you have to
be in their lives today.

*T*ell your family — Y.M.T.M. —
You Matter To Me.

*H*ome is not given, but made.

····*Mama's Rules for Livin'*····

*L*earn to laugh at yourself,

and you will never run out

of things to laugh about.

*P*ull together at home
as a team.

*W*hen you help your family,
you help yourself.

·····*Mama's Rules for Livin'*·····

*C*harity begins at home —

but it doesn't stay there.

$\mathcal{E}$ mpathy is your pain

in my heart.

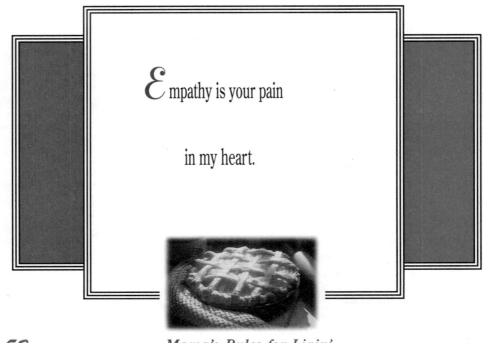

····*Mama's Rules for Livin'*····

$\mathcal{N}$o matter what's

happened to you...

I believe in you!

$\mathcal{D}$on't condemn, criticize,
or complain.

$\mathcal{F}$ix the problem —
not the blame.

····*Mama's Rules for Livin'*····

*I*f you speak kind words,

you will hear kind echoes.

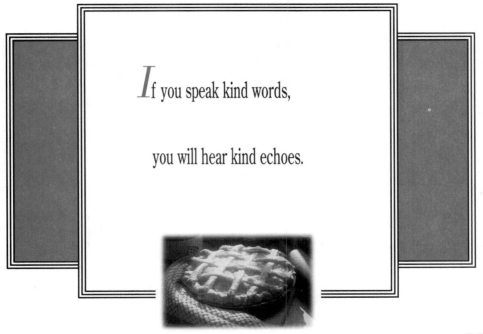

$\mathcal{P}$roblems become smaller

when you don't

dodge them.

·····*Mama's Rules for Livin'*·····

*P*roblems are only

opportunities in work

clothes...never quit!

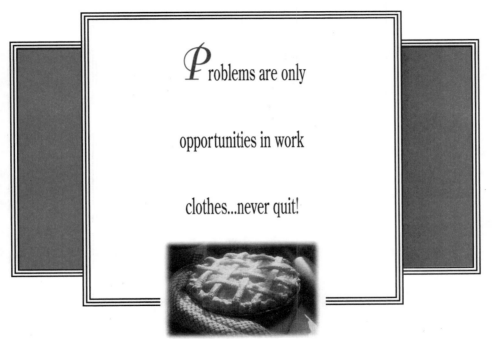

A gem cannot be polished
without friction.

T he child of God cannot
be perfected
without adversity.

*T*emptation is sure to ring

your doorbell, but you

don't have to ask it

to stay for dinner.

$\mathcal{Y}$ou don't have to *feel* good

to *do* good.

····*Mama's Rules for Livin'*····

*T*he good you do today may

be forgotten tomorrow...

do good anyway!

*I*t takes just one person to believe
in you for you to make it.

*S*uccess is always a joint effort.

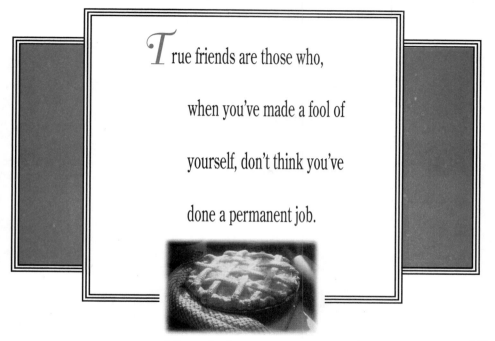

*T*rue friends are those who,

when you've made a fool of

yourself, don't think you've

done a permanent job.

····*Mama's Rules for Livin'*····

$\mathcal{T}$rials are opportunities to

prove God's faithfulness.

····*Mama's Rules for Livin'*····

*C*ome near to God and he

will come near to you.

James 4:8a

$\mathcal{K}$eep your heart right,
even when it is badly
wounded.

$\mathcal{A}$nger cannot live in an
atmosphere of prayer.

····*Mama's Rules for Livin'*····

$\mathcal{L}$earn to say kind things

because nobody ever

resents them.

$y$ou can regain your integrity;

it's never too late to start.

····*Mama's Rules for Livin'*····

When you become a parent

remember: Don't allow anything

in your life that you don't want

reproduced in your children's lives.

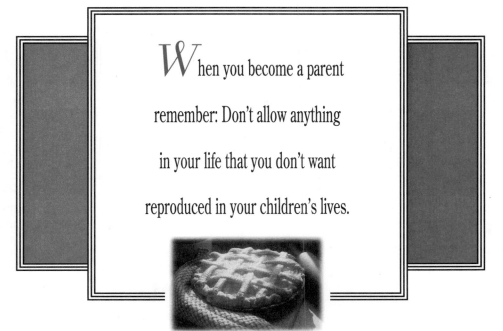

*T*oday is all you have, so live
each day to its fullest.

*L*earn to manage time,
energy, and money.

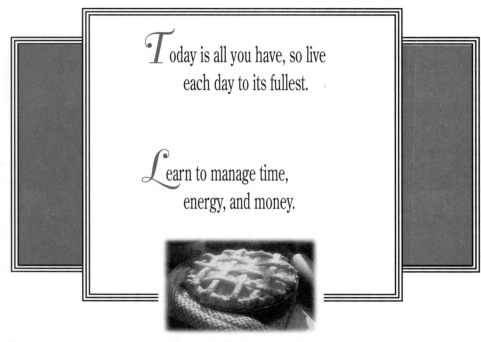

·····*Mama's Rules for Livin'*·····

$\mathcal{P}$ay who you owe, what you

owe, when you owe it.

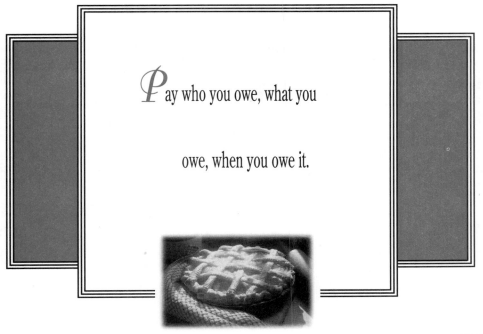

*P*ut gratitude in your attitude.

*F*ocus on your haves,
not your have nots.

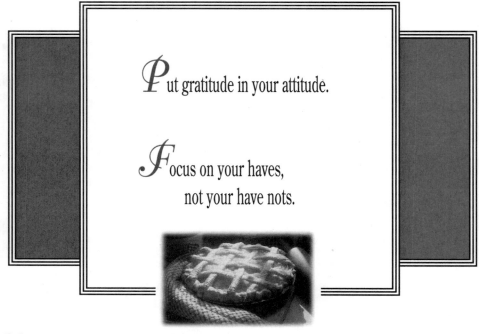

····*Mama's Rules for Livin'*····

*A*ccept compliments gracefully

and graciously.

$\mathcal{M}$ore and bigger

is not always better.

·····*Mama's Rules for Livin'*·····

*N*o matter your position or

lack of one...I believe in you!

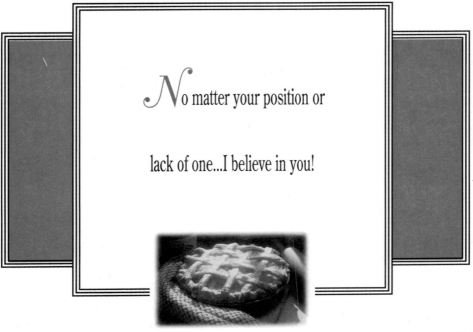

*D*ream the big dream
and go for it.

I *can* is a way of life.

$\mathcal{D}$on't tell anyone a problem

that they cannot help

you solve.

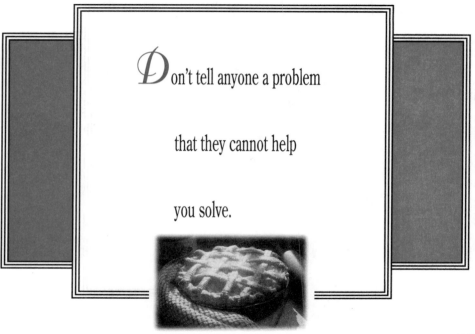

*A*lmost all major success

is preceded by defeat

or major adversity.

····*Mama's Rules for Livin'*····

*F*ailure is temporary...

never quit!

A cat may not have nine lives,
but *catty* remarks do.

*F*aults seem thick where
love is thin.

····*Mama's Rules for Livin'*····

*W*e are never more

discontented with

others than when we

are discontented

with ourselves.

$\mathcal{L}$ove unconditionally.

····*Mama's Rules for Livin'*····

*P*eople can be unreasonable,

illogical, and self-centered...

love them anyway!

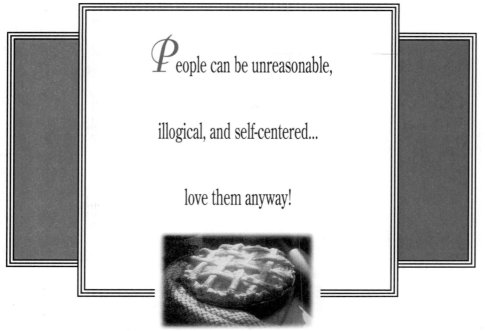

*T*he power to destroy
or build lies in the
power of the tongue.

*B*e careful what you say
to others.

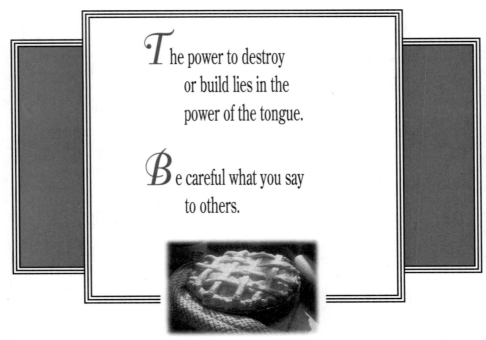

·····*Mama's Rules for Livin'*·····

*A*n apology is a good way

to have the last word.

$\mathcal{F}$ailure is a temporary event,

not a person.

····*Mama's Rules for Livin'*····

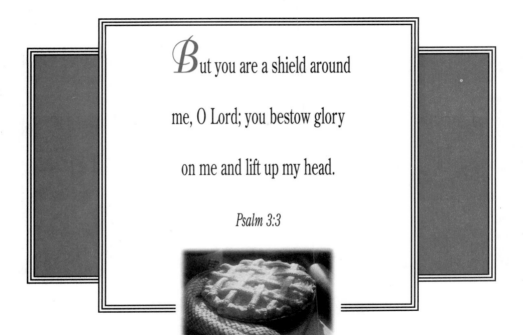

*B*ut you are a shield around

me, O Lord; you bestow glory

on me and lift up my head.

Psalm 3:3

Get rid of all bitterness.

"T" is the key difference
between a person who
is bitter or better.

····*Mama's Rules for Livin'*····

$\mathcal{T}$he person who is always

harping on something

is not necessarily an angel.

$\mathcal{U}$se the replacement theory

— replace negatives

with positives.

····*Mama's Rules for Livin'*····

When you become a

parent remember: Tell your

children you love, appreciate,

and believe in them.

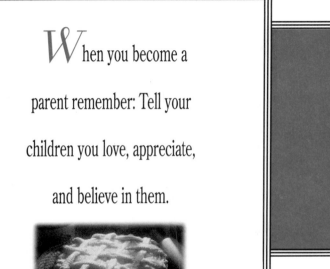

*T*hink quality in all you do.

*I*f it is right, it deserves
your best effort.

····*Mama's Rules for Livin'*····

$\mathcal{B}$e sure you are a part

of the solution not part

of the problem.

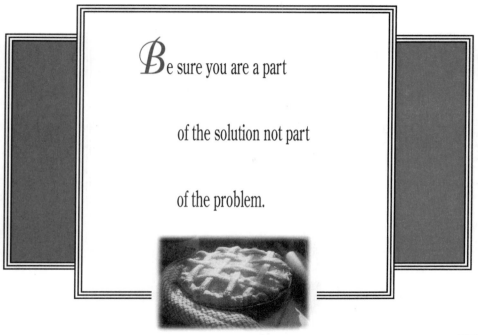

*R*emind yourself —
I've come a long way.

*E*ncouragement refreshes
the spirit.

·····*Mama's Rules for Livin'*·····

*I*t doesn't take a lot of muscle

to give a heart a lift.

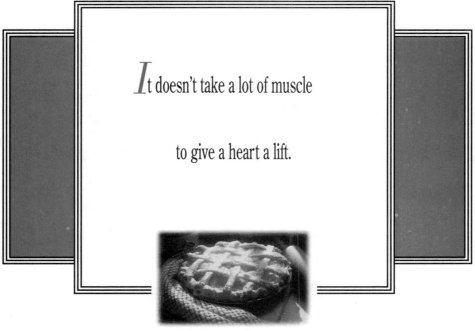

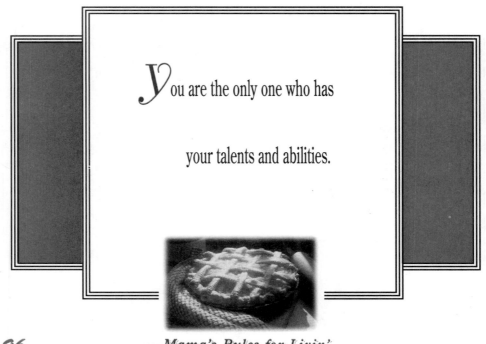

$\mathcal{Y}$ou are the only one who has

your talents and abilities.

·····*Mama's Rules for Livin'*·····

*N*o matter if you are

rich or poor...

I believe in you!

*U*se the most powerful
card you own —
your library card.

*T*he greatest unexplored area
lies underneath your hat.

·····*Mama's Rules for Livin'*·····

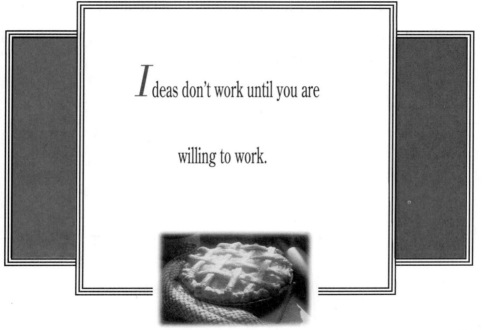

*I*deas don't work until you are

willing to work.

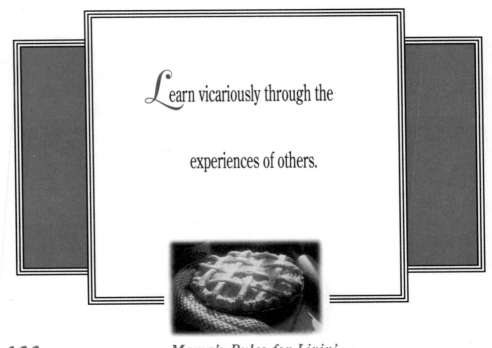

$\mathcal{L}$earn vicariously through the

experiences of others.

·····Mama's Rules for Livin'·····

$\mathcal{D}$etermine to be a world-class

person, capable of operating

in any arena of life...never quit!

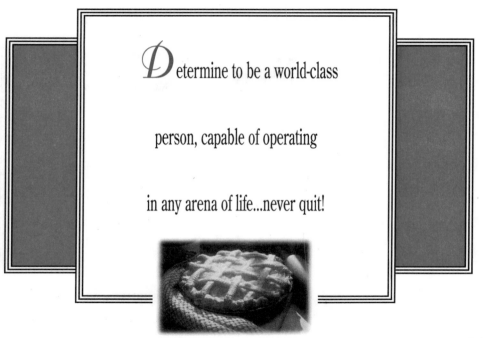

We become like the people
with whom we associate.

Select your mentors carefully.

*C*oncentrate on small

improvements.

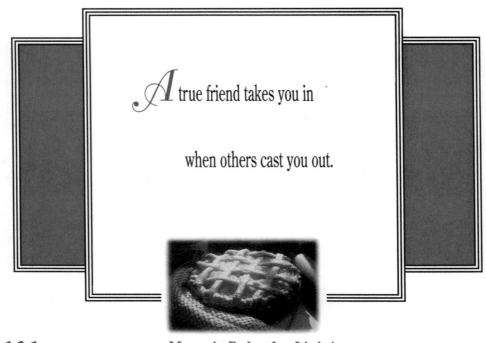

A true friend takes you in

when others cast you out.

$\mathcal{P}$eople tend to favor underdogs

but follow top dogs...

fight for the underdog anyway!

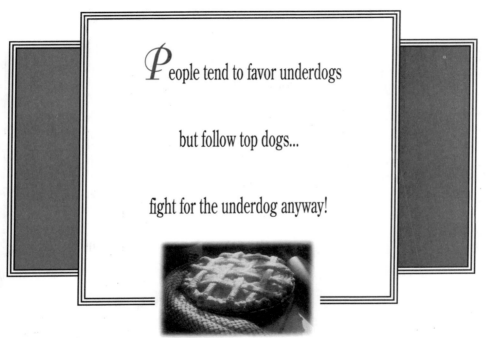

C onsider — how will you put your life together?

G oals are your roadmap to success.

····*Mama's Rules for Livin'*····

Goals, like eggs, soon spoil

unless hatched.

Work is not a punishment —

it is a blessing.

·····*Mama's Rules for Livin'*·····

Whatever your hand finds to

do, do it with all your might....

Ecclesiastes 9:10

*E*veryone deserves to
be understood.

*E*veryone needs rules
and limits.

·····*Mama's Rules for Livin'*·····

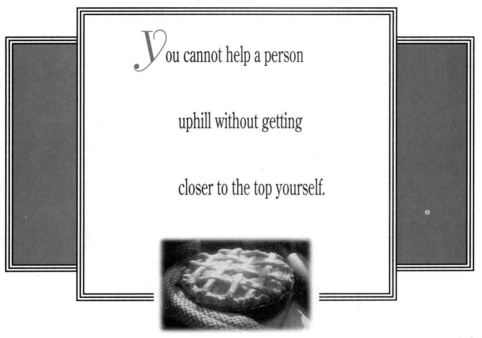

$\mathcal{Y}$ou cannot help a person

uphill without getting

closer to the top yourself.

$\mathcal{M}$aking a mistake is not an

excuse for living a mistake.

·····*Mama's Rules for Livin'*·····

When you become a parent

remember: Our children's

values will lay the foundation

for tomorrow's world.

$\mathcal{L}$ife is not always fair.

$\mathcal{D}$on't worry about what
you cannot control.

····*Mama's Rules for Livin'*····

$\mathcal{Y}$ou can have anything

you want but not

everything you want.

$\mathcal{A}$ttitudes are contagious.

$\mathcal{A}$ positive attitude will have
positive results.

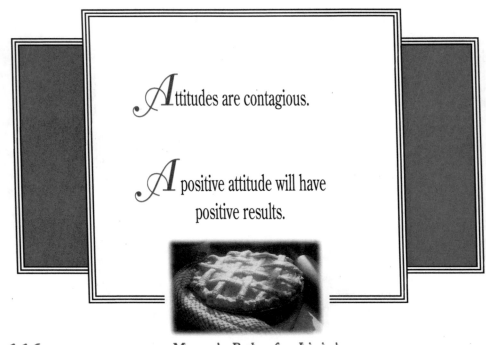

····*Mama's Rules for Livin'*····

*O*f all the things you wear,

your expression is the

most important.

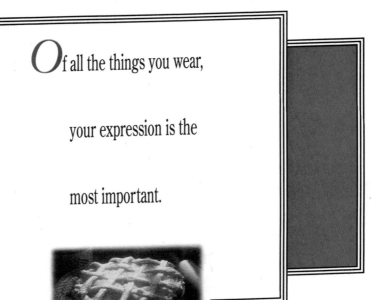

*I*f anyone speaks badly

of you, live so no one

will believe it.

$\mathcal{N}$o matter what others say...

I believe in you!

$\mathcal{P}$ain is inevitable —
misery is a choice.

$\mathcal{F}$orgive.

····*Mama's Rules for Livin'*····

$\mathcal{T}$he most beautiful gift you

can give another is the

gift of forgiveness.

*I*t is better to wear out

than to rust out.

····*Mama's Rules for Livin'*····

$\mathcal{F}$ailure and defeat become

permanent only when we quit

trying...never quit!

$\mathcal{K}$indness is a language
everyone understands.

$\mathcal{S}$andwich criticism between
thick layers of praise.

····*Mama's Rules for Livin'*····

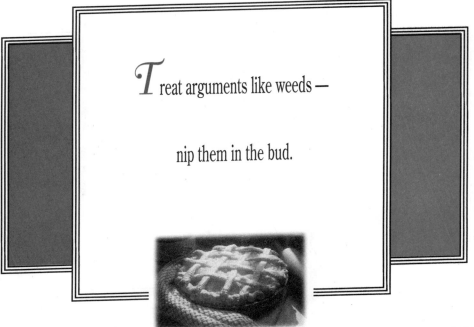

$\mathcal{T}$reat arguments like weeds —

nip them in the bud.

....*Mama's Rules for Livin'*....

What is down in your well

comes up in your bucket.

····*Mama's Rules for Livin'*····

*H*onesty and frankness will

make you vulnerable...be honest

and frank anyway!

*A*ct and look the best for the
people you love the most.

*T*reat your family as you
would a guest.

·····*Mama's Rules for Livin'*·····

*S*pend time with people

who are for you.

Gratitude is the memory

of your heart.

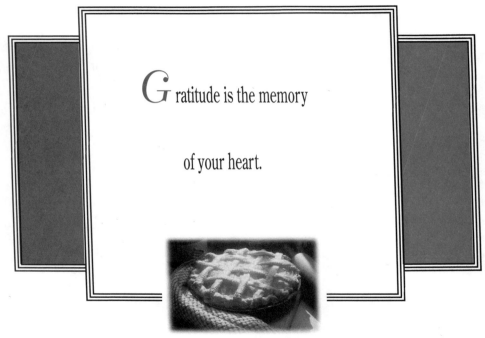

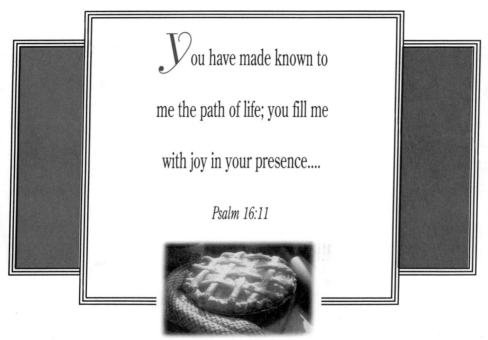

 ou have made known to

me the path of life; you fill me

with joy in your presence....

Psalm 16:11

*J*esus is the best model for
your home and marriage.

*G*od is the perfect parent.

·····*Mama's Rules for Livin'*·····

*I*f you wish to be loved, love!

·····Mama's Rules for Livin'·····

Get it together,

then remember

where you put it!

····*Mama's Rules for Livin'*····

$\mathcal{W}$hen you become a
parent remember: The best way
to keep children at home is to
make the home pleasant and a
place they feel loved — and let
the air out of their tires!

*Y*ou cannot put a band-aid
on a broken heart.

*N*ever break a heart
or a promise.

·····*Mama's Rules for Livin'*·····

*N*ever jest about another's

faults, failures, misfortunes,

or handicaps.

God may not always call
the qualified.

God always qualifies
the called.

····*Mama's Rules for Livin'*····

$\mathcal{B}$elieve in yourself.

····Mama's Rules for Livin'····

$\mathcal{D}$on't let yesterday's failures

bankrupt today's efforts.

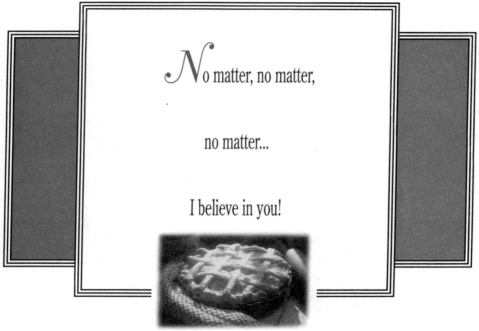

*N*o matter, no matter,

no matter...

I believe in you!

$\mathcal{Y}$ou are "thumb body."

$\mathcal{Y}$ou are a child of God.

·····*Mama's Rules for Livin'*·····

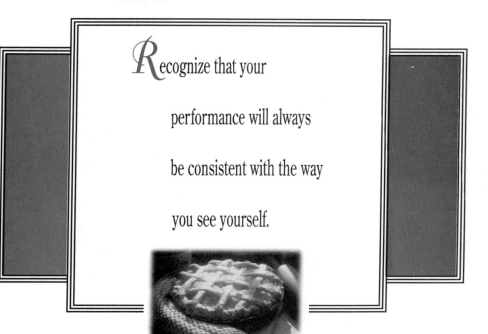

*R*ecognize that your

performance will always

be consistent with the way

you see yourself.

$\mathcal{P}$roblems become smaller

when you embrace them

as a part of life.

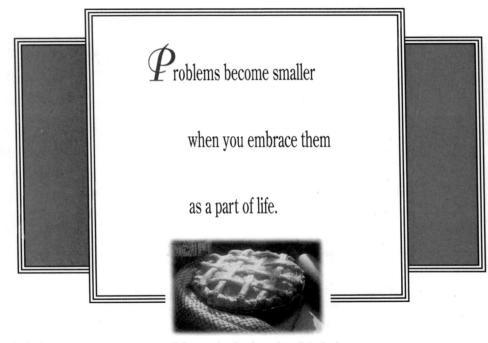

·····*Mama's Rules for Livin'*·····

$\mathcal{L}$ife is not one game —

it's a whole season...

never quit!

*R*emember that we become
real through love, maturity,
and understanding.

*T*hings invisible to the eye
are the most important.

····*Mama's Rules for Livin'*····

$\mathcal{T}$he largest room in the world

is the room

for improvement.

We all need love —

especially when we

do not deserve it.

*P*arents can be unreasonable,

illogical, and self-centered...

love them anyway!

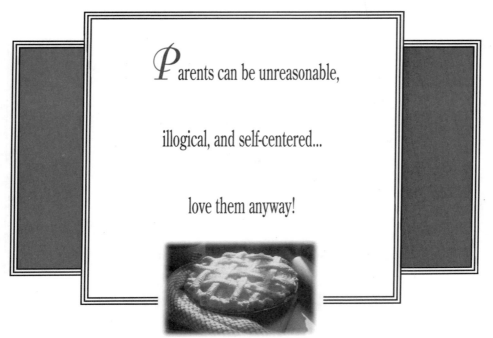

$\mathcal{R}$ealize that fear of the
unknown will never
be comfortable.

$\mathcal{F}$ace your fears.

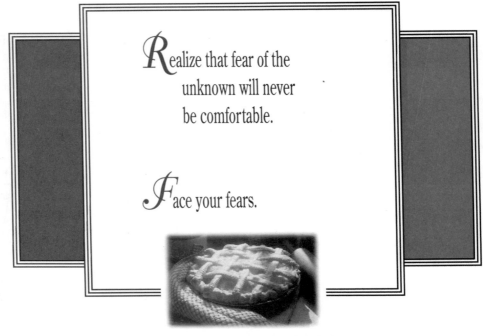

····*Mama's Rules for Livin'*····

*M*oving on is far more

productive than

hanging on.

G od will not do for you what

He has given you the

ability and talent to do.

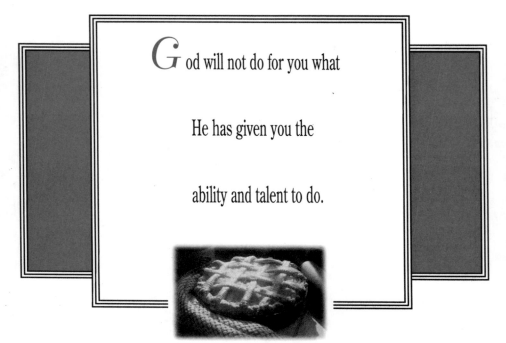

·····*Mama's Rules for Livin'*·····

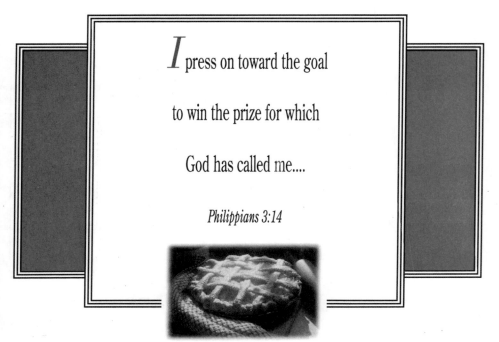

I press on toward the goal

to win the prize for which

God has called me....

Philippians 3:14

*L*ittle is much when God is in it.

*R*emember your label:
"Made by God."

····*Mama's Rules for Livin'*····

You may have had a bad start

in life, but you need not

have a bad ending.

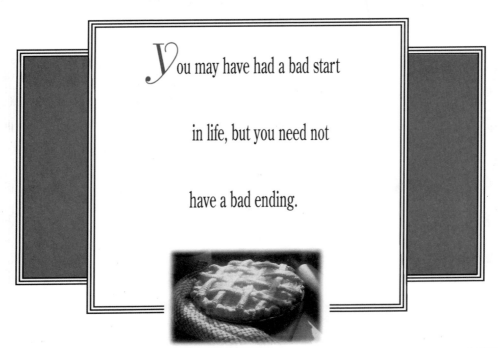

*I*t isn't *what* happens to you,

it's what you *make* of what

happens to you that makes

the difference.

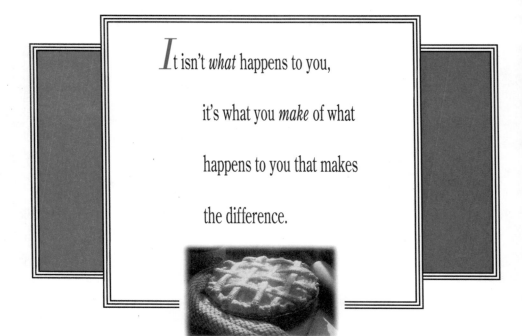

·····*Mama's Rules for Livin'*·····

When you become a parent

remember: If raising children

was going to be easy, it wouldn't

have started off with labor.

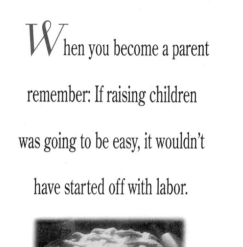

Mamie McCullough is one of the country's most popular motivational speakers. She addresses tens of thousands of people at churches, schools, and businesses. Having once toured with Zig Ziglar, the "I Can" lady now shares life-changing princi-  ples that are instrumental in providing women with ideas, suggestions, insights, and facts on how to raise "great" children. She is an encourager, business woman, author, educator, speaker and mother. Mamie feels her greatest achievement in life was receiving her M.A.M.A. degree.

Other titles by Mamie McCullough include:
I Can. You Can Too!
Get it Together and Remember Where You Put It

To contact the author for your
complimentary copy of her newsletter, *The Encourager*,
write or call:

Mamie McCullough
305 Spring Creek Village, Box 372
Dallas, Texas 75248
1-800-255-4226

Additional copies of this book and other portable
book titles from **HONOR BOOKS** are
available at your local bookstore.

God's Little Instruction Book Series by Honor Books
How To Be an Up Person in a Down World by Honor Books
Don't Wait for Your Ship To Come In by Honor Books
The Making of a Champion by Mike Murdock
Leadership 101 by John Maxwell
Momentum Builders by John Mason
Winning 101 by Van Crouch

P.O. Box 55388
Tulsa, Oklahoma 74155